THE HERMIT

DORIS CATHERINE PLANTUS

Lilac Publishing

Cover design by Doris Catherine Plantus

Interior book design, and eBook design
by Blue Harvest Creative
www.blueharvestcreative.com

This book is designed and formatted based upon the author's request for the speculative fiction genre.

SIHASTRUL—THE HERMIT

Published by
Lilac Publishing

ISBN-13: 978-1508410089
ISBN-10: 10:1508410089

FOREWORD
BY DORIS CATHERINE PLANTUS

Sihastrul (The Hermit), is the first in a series that in-
troduces the eponymous hero as an ambiguous character born under curious circumstances in mysterious cave,
but whose ultimate origins and destiny are determined
by much larger forces. The story is divided into books and
told from different points of view across a timeless ex-
panse from the very beginning of the world, to present
day. It is structured as a collection of apocryphal works,
(from the Greek word *apokryphos, meaning obscure, to hide
away*), whose themes offer a sense of innocent, if quirky,
ingenuity with which to reimagine the history of the
world. Its intention is to displace the reader into a realm
of possibility, a dimension of alternate perception.

The Hermit's adventures begin when the first breath
he draws coincides with an old angel falling from heav-
en, and sets a cycle into motion, though we cannot yet be
sure that this is the very first incident. The Hermit tells us,
"I began writing this tale *any* thousands of years ago...",
hinting at some sort of time travel. But the more intrigu-

ing proposition is that the Hermit adds, "maybe the words wrote me first, and now the tale set in motion continues to write and rewrite me. Now there's a thought." Therefore a number of themes are explored that question the way we understand language. The obvious point of origin is Genesis 1.

Although there are many biblical allusions, the novel has no doctrinal agenda. Instead, it borrows the scope and range of biblical literature for its original and refreshing use of language, breadth of theme, archetype, and plot, as well as its attempt to explain consciousness before the barriers of man-made science, philosophy, politics, and organized religion alienated so many other possibilities. Without a doubt, the novella celebrates creativity as a divine essence. It invites the reader to reflect on the human experience when imagination was its most tender and new, when consciousness — both human and Divine — began their relationship.

Finally, the literary innovation of super-scripted words in English, Hebrew, and Greek, mean to function as deeper possibilities of language. Like numbers, which are universal and infinite, language is a powerful creative force that does more than communicate an idea: it is evidence of our consciousness. It IS consciousness.

Admittedly, the novella is complex, but the addition of annotations can furnish the reader with enough grounding to make the work highly readable. In terms of influences beyond biblical literature, the style is magical realism, but the sort of which so many folktales possessed, long before a word described the style. Sihastrul was originally composed as a Romanian epic poem, in 2005, after which it took the form of a short story, before evolving into a novella. It was published as a bilingual version in an online literary magazine associated with the translation program at the University of Bucharest in April, 2013. Some of the challenges of the bilingual Sihastrul include sustaining the ambiguity of the Hermit's gender, which is never revealed, and coordinating the structural puns of the superscripts. For example, in English, the structural conceit of "sigh^{NAI}ed" is an allusion to Mt. Sinai, which can be rendered in Romanian effectively only by creating an adjective—"sin^{AI}tic". Countless other challenges abound in the difference between a gender-based language such as Romanian, and a neuter-based language such as English. In other words, the novella addresses translation issues if only in the mind of the bilingual writer, but would certainly resonate with other non-native-English writers, and the general public at large. I hope you enjoy the read.

Doris Catherine Plantus,
The Carpenter's Daughter

For Lucas, Andrei, Samuel, and Emmett,
so that you will always have me near.

BOOK I

I began writing this tale any thousands of years ago from most orientations in time, but not in the usual way, not in the usual way of writing and not in the usual way of time. I didn't so much write it as free the words from rock walls in a cave where I work silently, even now. Maybe I didn't write it at all; maybe the words wrote me first, and now the tale set in motion continues to write and rewrite me. Now there's a thought.

Language was first.[1]   It waited to be released from matter that had buried it in chaos.[2] I often wonder(ED) if there is(WAS) a word at the very center of this planet around which everything else has gathered; the further out from the center the more the words are layered, each one derived of the other, some melded, stacked, others blended, swirled, compressed, crushed, dissolved like memories proceeding from that one word.

Silently I work, almost tenseless,[3] in my humble cave chipping words from the damp stone lining, sounding

out the letters that emerge with each hammer strike.[4] S^H..
i^E..h^R..a^M... Now and then I wince from where the ringing chisel-sparks prick my face. I brush them away, they
smear across my cheeks and stain my face with subtleties;
always something is lost when words are moved from
one place to another, but they always leave tracks. I rub
the marks into my skin to initiate an obscure tradition.[5]

I cannot imagine someone will read my story, or if
it's already been read, and yet, it matters only that the
words be excavated, their meaning freed from the stone.
I like the idea that I $mine_{EXCAVATE}$ the words; it gives me
a sense of possession, a claim on history. Besides, the
tale is real only if it is written, otherwise, nothing can be
resolved, and nothing debated, nothing concluded, nothing fulfilled. Where there is no need to speak or write
language, there can be no time either. The weight of mor-
tality is the words we must spend before we die. Think
about it. There is no relationship to time until events are
set down. Language is what ^{CREATES}makes us live in time,
and makes us old, makes us remember.

So it follows there is no language without sacrifice.
There is no life without the telling of it, no way to
prove you've lived it unless you establish it in writing.
Otherwise, your life is nothing more than a bad dream
that makes no sense, cast off by someone else like wisps of
delicate butterfly wings. Nobody thinks very much about
that. But the many tears that have escaped me^{US} over this
point slide down the cool walls, and drip from the ceiling into prismatic spikes that hang like icicles from the
cave ceiling. Those same tears that drip down and form
icicles collect into puddles that coalesce, accrete, and
gather unto themselves into tapered speliothems.[6] They
congregate in caves fixed to the floor like sorrow when

it falls to its knees. One such large spike rises from the floor, remarkable in essence, energy, history. There are still other spikes, ones that hang from the ceiling, which belong, I think, to the rock; it weeps too, though I don't know why. Not yet. But they define, in part, the flat coal-color shapes that stick to everything, like shadows. When they touch the spikes they leave colored prints behind, like sight. These shadows. They mumble^{MURMMUR} as I work. They choose the words I carve out. S..I..H..A..S..T ..R..U..^{H..E..R..M..I..T}

I don't know who they are, the flat coal-color shapes. And I don't even know who I am, except that I don't hang from the ceiling or rise from the floor or stick to anything. But it feels as though it doesn't matter anyway for as many times as I've _{RE}lived this same tale, always from the beginning, and yet each beginning nested in other beginnings. I never even knew what I wasn't until I wrote the _{אוֹר}Word^{PHOS},[7] and it took a long time to liberate the letters, one by one. Each one is involved with what lays behind it; the letters are greedy and never satisfied, always wanting to be new words and say more, witness more, prove more. So there's no such thing as a simple story, for the letters compete for words, and words for meaning, and soon, even the shards and crumbs that succumb to the angle of the chisel, or the force of the hammer, might have inflected something else, had I struck with greater care. Sometimes you can read as much in my face, or see it in my eyes. Sometimes the birds mistake them for seeds — the rock crumbs, and snatch them in their beaks, then break into flight only to scatter fragments of letters. I have an idea that those fragments of letters dispersed by the birds can sometimes take root where they fall, and grow into words that make stories blossom at the tips of their stems, but not because they are really seeds. I think it is because the birds think they are seeds, and it is enough after all, if the birds believe it.

SIHASTRU[HERMIT]. It means "the one who is connected to the first word," or maybe, "the one who is free of the first word." I've mined many words that explain the memories that created them, but some have eluded me. Those that I couldn't free, or the ones that crumbled or chipped in ineffable fragments are secrets that many seek to discover, even in your times.

In all, there is only one other form that resembles mine though it never leaves the water. I think sometimes I am its shadow, except that I am not flat; it is. That's why, in part, I seldom venture out among the others who are different than me, except on nights where hot stars fall like fireflies that have stolen their light from stray sparks. I suppose they would think I am different from them, and that would make everyone uncomfortable. This is probably because they have not yet been named so they do not know what we mean to each other. No matter.

But today [WAS] is [WILL BE] a great day, so great, indeed that the fretting shadows easily peel away from the words that find their form — serendipity for them, fate, for me. The story begins this way, this time.

When the words had at last been carved, and the tale revealed, the moment came for my poor wandering mother to happen on this cave, alone and lost. I don't recall her features — how could I — but the shadows say that as she labored, the rock stretched and heaved until at last, I was away, slippery and strange. Then, in the instant I was to draw my first worldly breath as the offspring of a most capricious destiny that coupled with an unknown identity, it happened that an awkward angel began falling from the heavens. He was an intriguing character, by all measure of netherness; he slipped on a feather plucked from his side as he'd swept the horizon. Imagine that.

He often flirted with the edge of his universe, but at last, seduced by the earth's pull (for he claimed an intense attraction), he snagged the underside of his wing, close to his body,[8] on some trivial crag, made significant for the broken olive branch that yielded to a peripatetic dove.[9] At once his beautiful feathers that glistened with an ethereal unction known only to his kind started to glaze over with frost before quickly freezing altogether. One by one they turned to icy scales and burst into slurry-seeds hurled in all directions. Those below had said that on that day when the mysterious rain fell it made queer melodious sounds like broken brittle ^{MUSIC}glass. It was, however, a gentle, pleasant rain^{SONG}, and in places where the slurry collected, it formed interesting shapes, some quite large.

Well, the Angel lost his equilibrium, and just as suddenly, his appointed purpose. He arced in an unforgiving freefall, praying fervently for grace to recover his climb. Even now it isn't certain if it was mercy or punishment that attended his hasty prayer, because the sorrowful sigh that should have been his last, still full with everlasting life and compunction, rushed from his compressing body into my tender new lungs, precisely in the moment I gasped my first breath^{SPIRITUS}.

Thus at my first cry I wailed^{HOWLED} heartily, for I was a robust creature new with life while the Angel, pulled deep into me on the heels of his own desperate sigh, howled^{WAILED} in a curious arpeggio of emotion of so many octaves, that not one more note — not one — could ever be added. Why, there was scarcely enough room in my tiny being to host such a powerful form, so the angel groaned with discomfort at being squeezed into my soul.

Pop!

Such was our collective sound of blistered sobs and piercing screams that those who heard, remarked, "the babe must be bewitched to make this strange a cry."

In those days not even the soothsayer[10] dared speak the weird fate that awaited me, and some say that even God scratched his head just behind his ear saying He'd "...never seen anything like this before."

My poor mother never realized (nor did my companion) that all the time she suckled me the angel drank with such intensity —compromised as he was by being born^{re-born} this way — that he sucked the very life out of her. When my mother finally died, all that was left was dried milk on my trembling lips, for I had not drunk nearly enough. I cried^{HOWLED}. The Angel howled^{CRIED}. And the sounds we made, the two of us, so saturated the cave that my mother's shriveled shape dissolved into a small pool of our mutual sobs and whimpers.

The Angel's form surrounded my frail skeleton, and integrated itself into every vacuous place, increasing my mass considerably, and provided my tender muscles with radiant energy; I crawled without practice — a bit wobbly at first — to the edge of the pool, and lapped the cool water I warmed with my tongue. It made me sleep until I could stand, but all the while the Angel dreamed.

Eventually, I awoke to delicate, diminutive wings sprouted from my forehead — a sign of interrupted flight perhaps, and not so much a curse. Maybe more than this. I reasoned, such as I was able, that I would not be known for what I was, so by the time I learned the word *hermit*, I understood my relationship to time, the cave, the shadows, and the Angel besides.

Once I had grown bigger, my soul must have grown too, because the Angel howled less powerfully, being that his trapped grace now had room to stretch. And stretch he did, like a man who had been released from someone else's bad dream. Afterwards we got along a bit better, although he still complained of discomfort every time rain was imminent. He would moan and ask, "is it raining?" And the sound of the sky and wet drops on my face made me understand the meaning of the Angel's pain and sorrow. Such metaphors gave me to understand secrets that remained trapped, or shattered, although I could not make letters or words from them, yet. So we lived together in this fashion, sharing the same molecular space like mercy and punishment, or flying and falling; misfit and misbegotten, yet united in this spiteful metamorphosis of souls imposed one upon the other.

Of course, we learned each other's needs, and habits, or maybe we actually created them; I, how to steal away at night and milk the strands of moonlight that delivered the silver sustenance of his former paradise, and he, revealing where to find the purest dew that gathers in napping leaves. This replenished the immunity I had lost when he usurped my mother's milk, although I didn't know this until I sipped those first drops from the hollows of still leaves. He would say, "You're too little. Drink this, it will make you strong." Also he told me how to catch a lightning bolt by the tail without burning my fingers. I took it to be a useful skill, or else why would the lightning strike at all? Once I contrived to hide a lightning bolt in the cave with unexpected consequences. The lightning seared a vein of ore, and ricocheted everywhere. It scorched my body in a few places, and smarted despite my excitement, but immediately after, I spied a hammer and chisel glowing and hissing now white, now orange, now shiny blue. My racing heart rumbled through the angel, who was overwhelmed at the force, and thus persuaded to forgive me my poor judgment. He said, as an afterthought, "Don't ever do that again."

He grew more tolerant of my sort^{VERSIONS}, and there were even moments when I thought he liked me a little. I know he liked the way my tiny wings beat on my forehead. He would ask, "What's that supposed to mean?"

Whenever the Angel slept, I had great adventures in his dreams; once or twice I changed the endings, because when he smiled it gave me such a nice feeling. His dreams, you see, were apocryphal pastiches that revealed things before their naming, and I, with little else to bide my time took them for toys and amusement, instruction and revelation. I could taste what he saw, and feel what he heard; I smelled what he touched and touched what he felt — exotic sensations that resisted every feeble name I sought to conquer them with.

But he lamented, too, and of late, more and more. "Oh, what I wouldn't give to unfold my wings again and know the freedom of flight!" I don't know why it should have begun to bother me so, to be aware of his discontent; perhaps flying was just that spectacular that anything less would be worse than never having flown at all. I had seen many birds but never did I envy the way they soared so freely, especially the red bird. Not until now.

My brow began to mock me^{HIM} on account of those silly wings that could not lift me way up high. And one day so a great sadness came over me, and filled me so thoroughly that it filled the angel too until a strange perfume emanated from me. The tiny wings on my forehead began at once to beat furiously, spreading the perfume of my sorrow in all directions.

The landscape became blurred and aromatic, the leaves drooped as though they were melting and still the wings beat stronger and faster. I wonder now, had they been horns...

Suddenly I tore them out and threw them into the fire whose origin I would discover in another tale, but burned daily in a curious arrangement of rocks — neither circle nor square, but asymmetrical . They crackled for an instant, and changed the color of the flames, while from the wounds in my forehead clear nectar oozed into swollen beads, like the juice from plump, ripe, Thracian grapes.

It was a time of confusion, but it makes perfect sense now. The wings were not mine though they were clearly attached to me, and having torn[DEFIED] them without renouncing what they were, I had interfered with something ineluctable. So I ran toward the cave to wash my forehead and face[SHAME] of tears and blood and nectar but slipped without warning and fell precisely upon the prismatic rock that spiked upwards from the cave floor.

Imagine this.

The tip of the spike plunged *precisely* into the soft[SIGNET] raised mark on my belly, the most vulnerable spot [ΌΜΦΑΛΟΣ] on my body.

How could anyone know the pain[CENTURIES] that riveted through me, I remember thinking for an instant, and then I let out such a cry[WAIL] that the Angel, who surely profited from patience, was fortuitously expelled[LIBERATED] just as resourcefully as he had entered at my delivery all those years[SECONDS] ago.

Death lusted in that sacred space where prayer and punishment negotiate, but in that slow quickening of mercy and defeat my soul had seized the heel[11] of the Angel. As he soared upward from the depths of my being bound for the heavens once irrecoverable, he pulled behind him my own soul. At first I dared not let go, and then I laughed because I had no such corporeal concerns — no hands, no face, no eyes, no bone, no skin, and yet I crept over the Angel as he rejoiced in his ascent. The higher he climbed, however, the more he shivered, for he had lost his down with that first mystical rain. So I spread myself over him as best I could (he seemed massive). His trembling subsided a bit, but he said, "You're not very warm, now, are you. And I doubt you can cover the whole of me. You're too little."

Indeed it is a wondrous thing to fly.

But later, and higher, and farther out the Angel seemed to struggle. It was true that I scarcely covered him entirely, and yet the memories of all our time together seemed to impede his climb. The breadth of my soul barely reached the tips of his mighty wings, and still I insinuated myself into his bare structure with every lazy quark and surly muon.

Then I understood what had confounded the Angel's fight when he had sailed too low to earth. The draw of destiny from below and the profane weight of my soul throughout him had overcome him at last, and thus he[WE] fell.

• • •

But what of myself that chips away at the dense damp rock in this cave at the urging of shadows?

• • •

18

The pool of sobs and whimpers — the Angel's and mine — into which my mother dissolved had remained a living pool, though my mother was gone. When I fell upon the prismatic rock, the very one that pierced me through, my blood, mingled with the intrigue of the angel's essence, ran down the spike, splitting into curving ^{JAGGED} veins, and finessed further into the pool in a right-handed spiral. What cannot be resurrected, you see, recombines in shimmering strands of possibilities.

And the Angel sighed, and said, "It feels like rain."

BOOK II

After Adam and Eve ate from the forbidden fruit, the apple slipped ^{LEAPED} from their hands unobserved and rolled a bit, until it stopped a short distance from the accursed spot. The apple would have rolled on to infinity except that suddenly it became aware of its situation in the abrupt collision with a newly-born butterfly emerging from its cocoon.[12] The butterfly, naturally, was stunned, being tender with birth, but after a few ages he came around, though unaware of the time lost and the uncanny event besides. When he came to his senses, the apple had long vanished.

The butterfly blinked as if to freeze moments of evolution that had skipped over his unconscious slumber and compensated the comatose butterfly in the following mystical way: such an example of punctuated events would much later be called *deja vu*. Thus he *re*-emerged from a cosmic coma with the sense that he had lived this event before.[13] True, he was unsettled because the cocoon and the apple were nowhere in sight. But by and by his confusion dispersed, nevertheless, and misted the moon with strange dew.[14]

Soon he managed to climb freely in the air with nervous ease, as if only yesterday he was born in a tiny silk cave. Later on he found his mate (significantly advanced by now), and in her turn, she was charmed by the fragrance[15] of the apple that rose from the beating wings of the bewitched butterfly.

At the appointed time, according to heavenly custom, another infant butterfly emerged from his cocoon, only this one was fitted with little wings of apple leaves, rather than the diaphanous variety of his kind.

The curious little creature was delighted —if surprised— when on his first flight he had heard a harmonious melody produced by his beating wings. In a little while even the great God took interest and called the little butterfly before Him for a word.

"Say, kid, where did you learn to play like that?"

"What do you mean, my Lord?" he answered, playing his wings softly and clinging to a small branch that bobbed lightly so that he would not lift off in unexpected flight.

"These wings of yours — where did you get them?" God asked more precisely.

"From my cocoon, Your Highness."

And God, stroking his beard as white as milk, marveled and whispered to Himself:

"Why, I've never heard of such a thing."

"Are you angry, Master?"

"On the contrary," said He, smiling, "I kind of like it. Play some more."

And the little butterfly reprised the song from long ago in the future. Then God asked,

"What is the name of this tune, little one?"

"*Gugulan cu car cu mere,*" replied the tiny performer.

And then God sighed with such divine melancholy, that his sated breath sent the butterfly tumbling all the way to the back of the garden.

"Oh my goodness!" said God when he found the tiny butterfly hidden in some bushes, with his wee little wings tangled this way and that.

"Forgive me, Father's little one, I had forgotten how powerful nostalgia is."

And he straightened the so-small wrinkled green wings with His holy finger, and urged him there to perch.

And God saw that it was good.[16]

They say that many times since then He sought out the little artist and with a pure, immense longing, would say to him,

"Play that song that I like — you know the one."

In sweet obedience the little butterfly complied while all of heaven paused.

And God sang.

BOOK III

In the back of the garden an old Angel slept, stretched
out in his entirety on the grass that was as sweet and
soft as down. He was dreaming his favorite dream
where he flies fearlessly along the edge of the horizon,
like he used to when he was very, very young[NEW]. In fact,
he was the oldest angel precisely because he had chal-
lenged God in this way on more than one occasion, and
every reprimand cost him an advancement in years, according to divine physics, that is (which is, of course,
light years beyond the crude elegance of earthly physics); also the horizon was the very mystery of time, that
seductive ribbon that separated the mortal realm from
the heavenly. Nevertheless.

Every time the old-man-Angel dreamed his dream,
the LORD spoke to him,

"Mind your business — you know very well you are
not allowed to fly there."

And for good measure, the great God would let an apple or two fall on the Angel's head in divine sport, to wake him from his temptation. Then He would chuckle to Himself and hide before the Angel could figure it out.

This one time, however, the angel rubbed his head lazily, and drew open his mighty eyelids to discover there, on his nose, the tiny butterfly. He squinted, then focused, then spiked one eyebrow to an annoyed pitch,

"Hey, what do you think you're doing, kid?"

"Old man," the butterfly said softly, "won't you take me with you where you fly when you dream your dream?"

The Angel dusted the butterfly from his nose and assessed him more closely, as he hovered gently in the air.

"And how do you know what I dream, anyway?"

"Well," explained the little butterfly, "When I play that *doina*[17] our Father likes, he nods off, naturally, and then He talks in His sleep. Sometimes."

"Aw, who are you kidding?" replied the old-man-Angel.

"Honest. Word of honor."

The Angel coughed so as to hide the smile that stretched his mustache, in spite of himself.

"So?"

"So, He can't figure out why you do this. He mumbles that you dream while all the other angels rest quietly, and our Father doesn't like it. He says that it happened once before where wonder was confused with curiosity, and woe is them— well, you know the story."

"What story is that?" asked the Angel.

"The one with Aunt Eva."

Now the angel laughed without restraint at how the little butterfly could explain the matter so seriously.

24

"Our Father says that instead of marveling at the whole garden, she let herself grow curious about one forsaken apple, woe is her, and, well, there you have it."

"There you have it," echoed the old-man-Angel, "but what do you think you are doing when you ask me to share my dream with you? I mean, you said it — *curiosity*.

"Who, me? Why, I'm not curious at all. On the contrary, I marvel at it, is all — the *dreaming* part, I mean. Besides, I already *know* how to fly, but dreaming, that's the mystery."

The Angel was indeed impressed with the tiny little creature, how clever he was. And he agreed that flight is, in no way, a manifestation of so-called curiosity, or other words after that fashion (like temptation), since it was true that they could both fly.

"Let me hear you play something," said the Angel, and the butterfly shook his every part so briskly in his solemn preparation, that the vibration coursing through him ended in a *pop* in the key of "fa" at the end of his antennae. The Angel looked at him with circumspection and said:

"What's that supposed to mean?"

The butterfly paid him no mind and with daring poise he played so artfully that in a moment the old-man-Angel joined in, whistling leisurely, his eyebrows of silky astrakhan, undulating harmoniously at the will of the song until the very end of it.

"May you live long play and play as long as you live," said the humbled Angel, "you have a great talent in those tiny little wings of yours."

(They say that this is why so many Romanian folk songs begin with the words "*green leaf...*").

"Very well," announced the Angel, "let us go."

The little butterfly was so happy that his wings hummed with joy. "But you will climb on me first and behave yourself until we come upon one of those calm meadows. Get on my back."

Only the little butterfly was more daring than mindful, and scurried quickly into the old-man-Angel's mustache, weaving his tiny legs into the smooth silvery strands, and the Angel said,

"Hey--what do you think you're doing, kid?"

"UM–I–WS--CH.CH," mumbled the butterfly, as if his argument might be compelling even if the Angel had understood a word of it. Still he answered back,

"Don't be silly. You're too little."

But the little butterfly tac-flitted upward through the bush-wooly brows, provoking a mention of discomfort:

"Hey! That smarts."

"SORRY," replied the butterfly who, by this time, fled facially south and there wedged himself

beneath the silky thatch, firmly in those two vertical lines between the lips and the nose that have yet to be named, so the sound bounced into the Angel's nostril and echoed back into his ear. The left one.

"Suit yourself," the old-man-Angel quipped as he wriggled his nose, and launched into the celestial straits before he could feel the firmament rumble, for rumble it did.

They say that the old Angel and his tiny disciple took off in such a flight that even God could not imagine it, and they also say that He felt worse about punishing those two beings than He did when He banished Adam and Eve.

• • •

And so the old-man-Angel, together with his young friend, departed from God toward the brilliant meadow when, suddenly, they had gotten too close to the horizon...

Bad luck.

...and on a white-white feather that had snagged itself on the burr of the forbidden line, the Angel slipped and...

He did not call out from pain but from the cessation of the divine that abandoned him. Meanwhile, the little butterfly, who could not withstand the force of the fall, was driven into the Angel's nose, where he vanished into narrow cavities and plunged into a small oval structure with two lobes.[18] They fell.

And God cried.

BOOK IV

Anyone could tell you that the quill of the feather, newly plucked, hides the most delicate signature of life in its most pure, primordial particles. Similarly, it is common knowledge that the apple carries the recipe of its kind in its seed. When the forsaken fruit had collided with the tiny butterfly as it emerged from its cocoon, it had come to rest on the side with the chunk of flesh missing from its smooth surface against the floor of Heaven. The wound inflicted by Adam and Eve's curiosity, exposed$_{FREED}$ the very seed of sin which, heavy as it was with knowledge, burrowed through the firmament and fell in turn to root its place in the universe.

The affected apple, likewise, weighted with regret and promise^{HOPE}, profited from the hole bored by the seed ahead of it. It too assumed its place in the universe as a lifeless but mutable and charismatic moon, to provoke the after-souls of earth with the imagination and mood of its seed. The original bite can still be seen, though it lies on the side turned from earth. The angels call it *asham suf*, and it was once filled with tears.

Later still, the feather torn from the side of the old-man- Angel drifted, floated, rocked in lamenting motion until it urged itself in the apple seed which, stunned by the prick of the quill was moved to spin and grow by accretion of all the secrets that once mingled with the Angel and all he knew of God and Heaven, and then some. As the seed spun, the quill sank deeper and deeper into the center of its secrets; a burst of the lost kingdom was now trapped; around it swirled bits of the divine, and PERPETUALregret, culminating in mysterious unseen forces that would determine and define the earth (that's right; there was no big noise, bang or otherwise. More like a pop). The quill, therefore, became the axis, but even as it would be buried from sight, the feather strove toward heaven LOST until it broke through at the top of the world, which at that time was not north, but east.

The tip of the Angel's feather pushed forth slowly, firmly and sprouted in its unanimous solitude, glistening with toil and longing. Eventually, a tiny bud broke in the figure of an incandescent tear and salted the Earth with oceans of wisdom and remorse. Quickly new down gathered around the broken bud and there a single flower blossomed in consolation. The flower unfolded as it grew and grew, nodding to the eons that regarded it in passing, but did not wither, not even when it bent the feather clear to the ground. When the flower finally bowed and kissed the earth at last, like Virgil's poplars, so too did the feather release it and the new life$_{SEED}$ she carried. She would wander^{MAP} the earth for many histories in search of one particular cave.

Wherever she rested, she left behind a spring, and wherever she thirsted, snow-mantled mountains. When she hungered, wheat sprang from her footprints, and when she slept, the world slowed in its turning. Now and again she was given^{TAKEN} to dreaming and sweat-sand ran off her like powdered glass. She knew enough not to look back.[19]

What of the feather and the seed?

Her time is near, Master.

See to it.

Yes, Master. Shall we fill the hole?

And this gave the great God pause; he laid His finger upon His lips.

Not yet.

BOOK V

ANYONE WHO THINKS THAT MAN IS GREATER THAN THE EARTH IS A FOOL. BUT HE WHO IS HUMBLED BY NATURE SHALL UNDERSTAND FORGIVENESS. She saw this carved into the wall of the cave when she stood on the threshold. A sweet fragrance rose from a fire that burned inside a curious arrangement of rocks; flat black shapes flitted across the cold steam that warmed with every step she took further into the cave and fled in all directions. She slipped her feather cloak from around her and spread it on the cave floor, then she lay down upon it and fell asleep. The mountain sigh^{NAI}ed.

I remember being pressed from all sides; it was warm and wet, I held the firm and slippery rope with all my might. My head throbbed, something turned me this way and that, pushing me harder and harder, squeezing my soft bones and muscle against my organs. The silence was loud, shrouding the delicate cartilage of my ears with heaviness; I wanted to gasp, but a sticky viscous substance made me choke. Raw pulp suffocated me, stifled me until I was so compact, my atoms fused and then split. I burned with ice and shivered with fire, my body scarping the gelatinous walls of a tunnel engorged purple as I succumbed for a moment to an overwhelming surge of pressure that contracted my form toward an exaltation of cells.

My mind swooned when I felt the rush of cool air on my brow, and yet, something held me back.

The rope had coiled itself around my neck.

Bad luck.

As I felt the pull of the cord and the deliverance that seemed so willing to receive me, I had a clarity of mind that defies your science. I was in between one place and another, one set of terms and a different set of conditions, one reality and the next, an interstitial place called חיהNEANT חיה.[20] And like the folklore of so many cultures that claim a drowning man sees his whole life flash before his eyes, a creature in the *between* realm also sees his whole life flash before him, that is, the life that awaits him. This is the only place one can accept or deny destiny; if one gives up, it is here; if one refuses what fate proposes, here is the only circumstance where nothing is forfeited. It is not so much a question of a life not lived, as it is holding out for a different proposal. The catch is one must give up all one knows in that moment, to varying degrees, that is. So in this universe of the wondrous *between*, the self has many playmates, like *déjà-vu* and intuition, what you call *gifts* in all their miraculous range.

The Gordian knot[21] that held me fast demanded a more clever resolution than the strike of an ambitious sword — who would wield it anyway? The problem was *who* tied the knot in the first place. I could not turn back, nor could I appeal to the entitlements of biological processes that asserted their duties, right, wrong or indifferent. *I* had tied the knot because *I* resisted, because *I* twisted with fear and stubbornness, *I* let myself be distracted by the unknown, when I should have embraced my instinct to thrive, no matter what. No matter. I could tear the organ that had sustained me and drag it after me, put my mother in peril and let her see to my dilemma, or I could wriggle free as my tiny hand still clung to the rope. I knew my skull was soft and altogether slippery, perhaps I could pull my head out; better I don't. I knew that the life that flashed before me saw me strong and resourceful, capable of sacrifice and adaptation; I would not perish, I^WE will not perish, not here, I shall not perish, not here, not now. But there was simply no room to negotiate; I had to go forward and so I slipped my hand, then forearm, then shoulder into the white fibrous noose and let my mother's contraction propel me through the rest of the way. The ironic consequence of this move was that the cord was tied off before it was cut, therefore, the timing of my first gasp of air was perfectly synchronized to what happened next. The Angel's investment was so forceful, that it ruptured the cord to which I was still attached, tearing a bit of my tissue out with it. My worn and weary mother raised herself, stretched out her hand and pressed her finger to the hole in my belly that wheezed a strange light, that smelled of apricots, or almonds, and sealed the spot shut. The last thing I remembered of this particular birth was the pop in the key of "fa" and a voice saying,

Well, I've never seen this before.

BOOK VI

She is a funny girl, that one. She whistles to me as if she understands what I am saying by simply repeating my song. Sometimes she fancies she is a bird mystic and drops one or two notes from what I have whistled, to see if I will copy her. Humans are like that. They presume to be in touch with nature and understand its most precious secrets. How rude. Once she studied the grape vines that got tangled up with the pine trees and even wrote a poem about it, as if she was some kind of initiate with privileged insight into the natural, mystical world. I know, I watched her from the fence where I was munching on poison ivy berries. When she seemed totally enthralled in her study (and it was probably mean of me to distract her, but birds are mean, after all), I whistled and she whistled right back. Silly human.

And I must be a silly red bird to waste so much time keeping track of her the way I do. She thinks I am a sign that her father is near—and that's all right. Nothing disingenuous about that, just the human need for signs and surety that their faith is the best part of them, because actually, it is. Trust me. I come from a long line of portentous red birds, so even if I don't understand what she's up to with all this whistling, I know I am supposed to cross her path frequently and whistle to her even when she cannot see me. The funny thing is, we both know that what we are doing is important, only we don't know what *it* is. Go figure.

Today she is very nervous, anxious, pacing around the yard and going in and out of the house. I let her see me without whistling to her; instead I just make the color speak its brilliant red. She smiles at me. She doesn't whistle either, she doesn't have to. Today it's just about seeing. I show off a little and dart from here to there, rousting the branches and cajoling the leaves. Then I perch on the fence in full view. She gazes, really gazes deeply and I realize she makes me redder than I actually am. For a strange second[JUBILEE 22] I wish I could see myself the way she sees me. For an *enlightened* second, I take back what I said about this one; there is something very familiar about her, though I can't quite put my beak on it.

In my ancestral nest there are treasures. We live only 'round fifteen years, but our life spans are relative to the life we live. Our achievements are remarkable, even by your reckoning, but the point of my story is that in my ancestral nest there are treasures. I will give one to her because she made me more red than I could have ever imagined, so red that I was red even at night. *Essi est percipi*, says the Bishop.[23]

I flew to the sacred rookery and hunted through the bits and strands of history, woven here, packed there, until I saw the seed of a rock from millennia past; a speck of ore made a glint on one side — she would marvel at it, I knew it; she would make it more than it was. And that might be enough. It was snatched by my ancestors during the release of the Hermit's early mining activities. It is but a fragment, but a powerful one, on account of the word it was broken from, on account of the way the Hermit struck the rock. If anyone would know, she would.

She had aged by the time[24] I had returned, because I had to make the journey by way of degeneration, which is cycling back through previous generations in order to relay the object or message — in this case, the speck of ore — I was after in the first place. And it took longer still because I had to be sure I would re-arrive exactly where I had left off. I wasn't sure even then, you see, because many red birds seemed so much redder than I had recalled. But one look from her and my appointment was confirmed; I was still the reddest when she saw me cross her path. I honestly believe she knew it was me and not some other fool bird, though I had to admit that she herself had futured in ways I cannot describe. It was more than age, more than anything I could see. It was mysterious. Like she had lived a few lifetimes, not just the one. Anyway.

She whirled around, following me as I flew overhead, smiling and whistling that song she liked, and I, moved by this silly human, whistled back without thinking and let the rock seed fall from my beak $^{PRE}_{UN}$intentionally. She hardly coughed at all.

But she began collecting stones and rocks from everywhere after that, and even asked people who traveled places to bring her back stones.

"What kind of stone?" they would ask, and she would answer,

"Any kind will do — you'll know it when you see it."

You'd think they gave her rubies and diamonds the way she fawned over those stones. I'd see her through the window, taking them from her pockets and fingering each one thoughtfully. Then she would stack them in on the window sill, or on her desk — they were in every window, on every shelf, like standing stones in the desert. One she kept under her pillow.[25] So many stones — what could it mean?

She even took to building a wall of rocks in the yard from one end to the other, but didn't have enough to make it across. Instead she wound the wall around a maple tree. I perch there often because it perplexes me. The wall. But yes, she's a funny girl alright.

Then one day she brought home a rock the size of a melon. For a long time she sat on the back steps running her fingertips over it as though she were reading it, or trying to tell it something. For weeks she chipped away at one side of it, gouging out a hole so deep that it almost came out the other side. Her hair was a grey white like the color of that rock, and her fingers calloused and dry, her knuckles like the joints of poplar branches, swollen and gnarled. She looked tired and once or twice she coughed. I whistled to her but she didn't answer back; instead she took the rock with the hole in it and set it down in the middle of the yard where the grass was greenest on account of the way she looked at it. She lay down beside it and in a moment, vanished from sight.

BOOK VII

I dreamed I was on a strange shore that was beaten to a
blush by sun and wind, and in this invention of
loneliness was I barely discernible on a beach so indifferent to
me
and to the sun
and to the wind.
It was in a grey hour
       whose moment marked itself
against my profile in opposition to the passing of time;
I don't know anymore
precisely when I realized that
       my shadow had been missing but as I felt with my hand
the sand was cold at her last sojourn.
All hope then crumbled into grains of quicksand
into which my soul, heavy with passion slipped away,
       and I understood how small is man and how great is
       silence when you
       can hear the rattling of your own bones.

I awoke, finally, swaddled in a shroud woven as though by a
merciful spider, from the spindle of
      forgetting
conscious with every blink of my eyes that burned with sleep
and wind
and sun that any movement would collapse me into salt and ash.
I felt my frail breaths through the tightening and loosening of the
cloth that began to tear from this profound release;
      I sensed myself so close against the
            breast of neant that the space I began to fill with
            my pathetic, withered form
was not part of the molecular plane of time's movement. I was
embraced and yet not integrated
in this place damned by the sun and
the wind and
my soul sequestered in this forgotten beach.
      Where once I was spiteful of tears that
      fell as though for no reason, where I was once spiteful of
      all the love
that was contiguous with my body and being when I
      loved you.
      I am now spiteful of this forsaken spot that mocks me
      with the contradiction
of my existence.
      I fell asleep.
      I am now spiteful of this forsaken spot that mocks me
      with the contradiction
of my existence.
I fell asleep without struggle or remorse, rocked by my bones that
beat like the
      sound of the toacă[26] towards midnight,
and I dreamed I wrote your name in the sand
and the wind slowed, and the sun left off,

and the swaddling began to melt in
    muscle and meat and nerves upon me like a
    living cipher.
The waves approached this strange shore resurrected by the sun
    and the wind, like regrets,
    and I understood how small is the pain of sorrow, and
    how great
is need, when you can still cry beyond death. And it was then I
wept a tear—
    a single, hot tear that turned the sand to a glass bottle
    where it fell; and into it
I poured the sleep
and the dream
and the death of this shore,
this shore so indifferent to me
the sun
and the wind.
I hurled it toward the horizon, toward you, toward the west,
    and the farther the sea carried it, the smaller this cursed
space became, until my soul
long buried, rose toward the sun. After, I awoke on a strange
shore, beaten to a blush by
the sun and
    the wind,
    and I found your name written in the sand. I sat down
    beside it, and fell asleep
and dreamed that you once loved me.[27]

BOOK VIII

W e stood on the deck of the mighty ship, the copper and olive tones of our skin resonating against the ubiquitous blue scale that surrounded us. They say that all the possible shades of blue in the humanverse can be found here, which is to say, along the route we sailed *this* time. The nature of our expedition was simple: we must catalog each species of blue in the realm of color. We had an obscure map with crude but charming symbols and amorphous land masses that lacked sharp   clear   lines, crowded   together   on   the   soft[FRIABLE] palimpsest, heavy and given to crumbling like pastry dough when we un-rolled it. We were making for the straits of Voronef[28] blue — that breathtaking 15th century generation of ultrama-rine, heir to lapis lazuli of certain dynasties who knew how to mine colors, tap their roots, draw them from the earth, deep in the center from the kingdom trapped ages and ages ago[HENCE].

The wind buffed the sky until the horizon line suffused with the sprawling seas in all reaches. We broke the water's plains with our ship that squeaked and rocked in soothing repartee with the pitch-strained seams of its groaning hull, and felt our soles[SOULS] anchored firmly to the planking. We sailed on periwinkle oceans beneath a cerulean sky, but the very air we breathed as we neared the Great Band was now *Voroneţ* blue. And the sea for us became a monastery of wonder and wisdom, and the salt was sorrow.

I leaned over the side, and saw the gridlines that lay deep in the water. The Blue Route is one of the few places left where one can still see the lines by virtue of the beam of light that radiates out from the center, and this, only because there is a tiny hole there in the shell that surrounds the trapped kingdom, with very mystical origins (both the kingdom and the hole). The water was so pure in its color, that the finest gradations of the lines were visible: a vast gossamer net projected from the earth's *center of moments* over which we ran like a spider, sticking to the spring-loaded silken strands of its web, our sail-prints rising like silver foam in our wake.

Just as we crossed the Great Band a powerful jerk seized our ship as though we had run aground or suddenly dropped anchor, dragging us to a thrashing crawl. A desolate expression overtook my father's face and he said,

"We've lost the longitude."

The implications were horrifying beyond the mere loss of position, making navigation dangerous if not deadly. More than this was the collapse of the gridlines that sustained the force fields of earth and, particularly relevant to this accounting, the rather poetic force of *relative* gravity.

How we lost the longitude was impossible to conjecture; rather we were presently distracted by a resumed movement, a laborious thrust with the most dire of sensations— we were circling the lower half of the world like a toy boat circling a drain. The only other thing my father said to me was this:

"We must find the longitude." What he really meant was *I* must find it.

My eagerness to hope mingled with my youthful desperation and in an instant I was so removed from our present circumstance that I saw the Earth from a vantage point in space. I saw the ship — upon which I was still standing next to my father — spiraling down gracefully, steadily, to the bottom of the world, where I knew we would simply fall off. I could see it in stunning detail. On deck once more, my fear was ironically casual by now, muted by the omnipotent force of *relative* gravity pulling us downward, ever downward, and the further down we circled, the faster we descended.

Yet it seemed to take forever. I saw the history of blue flash before my eyes, and the veritable journey of fear that took me from the deck of our vessel into deep nether-space and back again. *Esse est percipi...*

You have learned to measure all things by numbers. You have let yourselves be misled by pious buffoons and social architects who build their world of reason around the premise of a system of number writing that boasts neutrality and universality. They fuse logic and infinity so that we may establish the mind in a cerebral paradise where many are excluded, save the seasoned scientist. (Quite the opposite notion of a mansion with many rooms, but I digress). They have made us a race of quantifiers, imposing mathematics on everything. But this is a ruse whose invention proceeds from vanity, because numbers, like words and colors *precede* us.

Scientists merely mimic numbers without truly understanding what they sound like, or what they really mean. If I told you now, that the very spot from which I perceived our mighty ship was the end of *pi* you would understand that it was also the beginning, so when I had returned to my place on deck, I brought with me the last number in the infinite span of integers; it was enough to arrest the ship, or maybe even the earth as it turned, and grind it to a halt. In the instant my father's eyes and mine locked the earth began to spin the other way and raise our ship in greater rings of circumference, back toward the Great Band, knitting the frayed longitude after us. Pole shifting has happened many times, indeed. But what you haven't yet contemplated is the reversal of the earth's rotation, as explained in the Book of the Trapped Kingdom.[29]

If my father's expression was consumed by desolation it now shined with redemption. I remember now that we didn't speak anymore after that, nor after we made port and I scrambled to shore to feel the ground beneath my feet. I took a few steps besides, to feel the certainty of the earth upon which I stood. And from where my father watched on deck, he saw that it was good.

BOOK IX

I looked upon my newborn babe, squirming and fretting, shining with life. I wiped the tiny body with my feather cloak and suckled my infant whose appetite was great. The ruptured spot that I had sealed with my finger was smooth and delicate, a signet, slightly raised but healed, a stamp of virtue culled from the husk of the apple seed before its integrity was breeched. After three days of vigorous feeding, I swaddled my child who now slumbered in a nest of feathers I wove from my cloak. The curious object expelled from inside me after the babe was delivered, lay motionless, still attached to the white fibrous cord with a knot at the far end. So I dug a hole in the floor of the cave and buried it, as if the knotted cord would take root.

But take root it did, for in my final moments, when my life flashed before my eyes, I saw a stain spread over the spot that still bore my handprint where I pressed the damp earth over the hole. The knotted bulb burrowed deeper and deeper, now a juggernaut, now an avatar seeking out itself. And the displacement of bedrock and mantle churned behind it, disrupting the geosphere, but the strangest thing of all was the stirring of my handprint and the raising up of one finger from the print, with a signet branded on its tip.[30] I called out to my child and whispered a prayer of mercy and thanksgiving, protection and humility, courage and compassion, forgiveness... yes, that too. And my voice remanded every letter of every word that gave the sum of my life and history in purchase of my death to the secret cave.

BOOK X

Raphael lingered often by the hole in the firmament. Sometimes he peered thoughtfully through it, pushing aside the silver mist with his hand, for such a mist was necessary to conceal the hole, which from earth, looked like a cloud; other times, he pressed his ear to it.

He's at it again, Master. I told you we should have filled it long ago.

The great God was taking a stroll, humming a tune with his hands clasped behind his back. He slowed a bit but kept strolling, and said,

Calm yourself, Michael, all is as it should be.

He's not the only one, you know.

Oh, I know.

Then?

God gestured to Michael to come closer and Michael drew near in earnest.

I told him to keep an eye out, and an ear open...

Michael shook his head and smiled in a slightly insolent way, and said,

But we can do that without the hole, Master. Raphael seems bewitched by it — truly he does. It's dangerous besides. Why, just the other day I tripped and nearly fell.

Oh, come now, Michael, you will never fall, you cannot fall. You are right, though, we do not need the hole.

Then?

HE needs it.

Michael was incredulous and laughed out loud.

You can't be serious — him?

I don't like your tone, Michael.

Forgive me, Master, I mean no offense, but really now, you don't actually believe it is possible after all this time?

Oh, dear Michael, all things are possible — and then some.

Meanwhile Raphael was peering so intently that he did not notice the edge around the hole giving way beneath his knee. Before he could fully appreciate what he had set into motion, all of good intention, God and Michael had arrived and appeared consternated. And God said:

Uh-oh.

At this Michael and Raphael were struck with rigid reckoning, Michael's hand was set to draw his mighty sword, while Raphael smartly assumed the posture of a noble volunteer for a deadly mission.

Just kidding, said God with a disarming twinkle in His eye. Then he patted Michael's hand till he let go of the hilt, and promptly boxed Raphael on the chin.

The firmament you loosed in the exercise of your divine duties, namely and principally, listening to prayers, is evidence of the answer I shall give, for there are dark days ahead where

the people will call out, and by then, what you have loosed with compassionate [IN]attention, will fall like manna from heaven.

On the outskirts of heaven a sky of brooding violet came down around her shoulders; star-dappled folds crowded her breast as she hovered in the doorway. She thought of the child she'd left behind in that cave and the grass beyond her stoop began to fret beneath the evening dew. A wandering rhapsody wove each blade with such variations on an august night in her memory that it ran along the rings of heavenly spheres. From this threshold she studied her child's movements, gestures, limblines, her soaked and anxious pupils breathing the cool white down that spread over that altered but handsome face. Once or twice the child paused, as if sensing she were near, perhaps her smile, winging on the wake of her gaze like aromatic lace falling just out of reach. She watched with mixed longing tracing the features of the youthful Hermit, aching to stroke the ripe curls that framed the taut forehead, from which fanned the tiny wings a sweat that sprayed aloft the brow as the hammer struck. And struck. She leaned into her shadow to ease its trembling and the summer pear she held in her hand transpired, dispersing its fragrance. She wept and retreated into her Rookery, for this was the place where red birds bred and nested and kept their treasures.

Do not weep so. Gabriel spoke to her, but she heard him not and let the pear fall from her fingers. And Gabriel took pity on the calloused hands of the woman who had wandered for ages and ages, sturdy and plain, not soft, not fierce, but resolute and obedient, after her kind.

Then a sound at the casement distracted her from grief and there she found a pebble on her sill.

It was an unremarkable little pebble, scarred, pitted and unpretentious it seemed to her; she fingered in her palm what Sappho[31] recounted having dreamed. The light of the moon grew like hunger baring the ribs of midnight in anguish:

"Will you speak to me, my precious pebble and earn my gentle heart? For I cannot leave my Rookery until I've filled its every room," said the mournful woman.

The pebble was steadfast silent though she sensed an energy there, so she drew her private bath and tied her sparrow-grey brown hair. The water steamed by starlight sizzling like arctic rain in the hollow of her chest, against such dancing beads of longing the tiny stone she pressed.

Now a mist rose all around her and seeped into her so that the beating of her tender heart pumped throughout her the pebble's soul. Her earring turned to whispers, at her neck locks splayed like bulrush, and the last drop of stone released at her shoulder, left behind a purple blush. The pippin[32] stone thus vanished, the night air rushed about her. But outside her rocky keep a lightning drenched horizon made a lodestone of the moon, and so too a quickening spread beneath her breast. The moon climbed higher still and pulled so resolutely at her heart, that her shadow — her very shadow churned and sprayed hot foam and minerals.

At last her gentle heart burst into shards of self and longing, and of the pebble, a lost forgotten sorrow scattered at the Hermit's feet.

"Why, it's only broken pottery," said the Hermit, who noticed the fragments among the grains of chiseled stone on the cave floor, "and yet how strangely fragrant; perhaps a common vessel, that one time held a pear."

BOOK XI

Each time they fell together, the Angel and the Hermit, the puzzle was magnified in slightly altered ways. This time they streamed across the sky of resplendent ultramarine on the occasion of the very first rainbow, diverting the colored bands into a trajectory that included part of one very important promise.[31] They splashed down into a marvelous sea of such brilliant blue and intense curative properties, that the Hermit's soul, previously stiffened into an exoskeleton that nearly covered the Angel entirely, was lifted from every bonding point like a translucent film and promptly floated toward the surface. The Hermit, starved for air like a shipwrecked mariner folded and unfolded the stunned soul a thousand times, reefing it this way and that until the rush of cool air soothed the wingless brow and the Hermit's body was restored. Looking in all directions for the some sign of the Angel, the Hermit quickly dove several times in search of the old companion, but to no avail. An object then appeared in

51

sudden view near a mighty ship[32] that listed despairingly as though having been heaved and battered by unimaginable forces.

The Hermit swam first toward the ship but then decided that the object, nodding as it sank, would soon slip beneath the shimmering surface of the anonymous sea. By the time the object was plucked from the folds of the water, however, the ship was now nowhere in sight. The Hermit drifted for many days, and eventually lost consciousness, but held fast to the object even so. The waves yawned gently at first before buffeting the Hermit to the waiting sand.

For several more days the Hermit lay face down on a strange shore[33] that was beaten to a blush by sun and wind, and the silence was so great the Hermit could hear the very rattling of bones. A red bird aloft sailed like a kiss thrown from a railway platform, carrying a stray morsel of sustenance in its beak. When the Hermit rolled over and gasped in such a familiar way by now, the red bird dropped the morsel and the Hermit barely coughed; the object retrieved from the sea's breast was still secure in the white-knuckled hand that would not it let go.

The object? A leather pouch.

The contents? Five small sticks and two stones.

The meaning? To build a kingdom.[34]

But how? How indeed!

The Hermit was strong, supple of limb, sturdy and plain but radiant in purpose, skilful with the most primitive of tools, gifted with the art of invention and design. The two marks on the forehead continued to weep the peculiar nectar that oozed like the robust juice of plump ripe Thracian grapes into cupped and steady hands, though calloused from toil. A bottle had washed ashore as though tossed from someone else's dream and into it the nectar was poured carefully until the bottle was full. The Hermit drew the plan of a fortress in the sand with one stick, and placed the remaining four in the corners that marked the main palace, then sipped from the bottle and fell asleep. After the Hermit awoke the four sticks had become now a framework of buildings and towers, churches and monasteries — a structure beyond comprehension, intricate yet simple, lying in a triangular plane with gardens and streets. Then the Hermit set the stones in two opposing diagonal corners, drank from the bottle which was still full as at first, and slept once more.

This time when the Hermit came to the two stones had transformed into vast high honey-colored walls that filled in the wooden framework. After this the Hermit poured the bottle of nectar into the sand and added sea water to make tiles for the roof. The sand turned blue from the water, was kneaded properly and then formed into squares, and after, pressed and shaped around the top of the Hermit's thigh, then left to bake in the sun.

When it was finished the Hermit took the first stick that scribed the plan in the sand and wrote these lines on the strange shore:

Every heartbeat,
> *a grape blossom,*
> *every grape, a glass of wine and*
every glass of wine, a sea in which the stars bathe.

> *Four drops of rain make*
ten brass nails, and ten brass nails,
a kingdom where the
> *king tends sheep.*

A twinkle of the eye, a secret
      slipped like unstrung beads; every bead,
      a moon forever full beneath whose light I sleep in
your arms once more.

and then walked into the sea.

BOOK XII

I noticed she was missing^{STOLEN} the minute I walked into the kitchen. He tried to hide the deed by bragging about how clean it was, the kitchen, and indeed it was, but the empty kind, so I wasn't impressed.

My heart walked over to the counter next to the sink to have a better look. Yes, she was gone, alright. Other things were missing too — a spice rack from my mother, with full bottles of pulverized seeds, rumpled sage, slivered rosemary and garfunkeled-thyme,[37] stiff warped bay leaves with missing pieces and faded stubble of parsley, more yellow than green. Spiky cloves. But even so, it was a gift from my mother. Gone. And the bread box that was too small for serious bread, whose door stuck besides. I used to put silly things in there like tiny brown bags I had folded neatly (in the event that I would need such a bag, but never actually did). Also gone. It's true I couldn't remember just how many utensils stood like a slanted bouquet with wood and stainless steel stems in a stout ceramic vase, *but the spoons* — those worn wooden spoons, the smooth handles that loved the touch of my grandmother's fingers when she wrote stew, or scribbled sifted flour into hot oil with minced garlic, propped one against the other in that ceramic pot — not there. I moved aside with my eyes the indifferent square sponge and the sink with the dull blameless finish; the wall shined as my eyes rolled across it, so now it was obvious that she was simply not there.

"Hungarians are clean," he said with magnificent tone. I can't remember a more oppressive heat in July. The air was mushy, the molecules like invisible fish eggs clumping against my skin, making me heavy with despair[SWEAT].

"Where is—"

"I don't know. It's clean. I made it clean, see?"

"But where—"

"Hungarians are clean. When I was a child, I was always cleaning and even my mother, who was also very clean, thought I was strange because I was always cleaning. See how nice it looks? *Clean.*"

His mother was right.

He turned away. He did not answer. He did not see my heart on the counter, or my eyes on the wall. I took the rest of me and went looking in a loud sort of way.

"I put it over there. Somewhere," he said, as if giving a grand speech, pointing his thick fingers in the direction of a tiny room off the kitchen.

I saw the spice rack and bread box huddled together in a cardboard box but she wasn't with them.

"Maybe I threw it out," he added with such hollow intonation that it echoed in my chest and eye sockets. *It.* And a smell like blasphemy made rancid curls in the air.

It was Tuesday afternoon, which meant the garbage that had been hauled to the street some 400 feet away had been simmering in the hot sun all day. I hate garbage with an unusual zeal because the raccoons routinely get into it, gleaning the sordid contents with wild abandon, which means I am forced to spend time with it — the garbage — raking it, flicking the far flung particles of stained wrappers and dead vegetable peelings back into the can. And the smell...

This was different, however. It was 96 degrees and muggy. I could hear the garbage truck a short distance away so I hadn't much time. I could feel my heart and my eyes looking after me from the kitchen window. I left them behind the way you do children who need to be protected when you say "Wait here."

There they were, four large rubbish cans in a neat row along the side of the road. When I lifted the flaccid plastic lid off the first one a burst of stagnant warm putrid air hit my face.

My nose diverted the function of breathing to my mouth as if to spare my lungs the sickening odor, so the noxious fumes dove straight to my stomach, as if I could fool my own brain into thinking the stench didn't exist, simply because I had bypassed the olfactory. *Esse est debeat?*[38] Quickly, I hunted through the smelly foam gurgling from sagging fruit and rotting tomatoes scraps. I hadn't had time to bother with gloves or even a shovel — anything but my fingers. Fingers it was. I didn't find her. I opened the second can and it was drier, but no less disgusting.

Half I emptied into the first, sifting through the refuse like the raccoons that vex me. Nothing.

The third can of garbage was wet and ugly, soft deformed rinds of melon, withered seeds (I had a dove named Noah), sticking to my hands, papers damp with condensed swill of mingled juice and slime. She must be in the last one. *She.*

What was he thinking? Who does this kind of thing? I was incredulous, but I was hurt too, yet more sad than hurt, more hurt than angry. I rummaged through the fourth can of garbage, feeling nausea in my mind and a burning in my bones; there, at the very bottom beneath some gnarled chicken bones was my icon of the Virgin Mary on a long key chain with a fish. I should explain the fish.

When my sons were young we had a little aquarium, and gave names to all the fish. I chose Lucky (though they all died). For my next birthday they bought me a fishing lure and said it was a *lucky* fish.[39] So I removed the hooks and wore it on my key chain. Over the years I received many more lucky fish so that in a while they were everywhere, attached to things of importance, or not. It happened that I had a very long key chain, and a very long lucky fish that I put on it. It used to hang on a nail on the wall in the kitchen, important unto itself, until one day I put a silver icon on it too. Then I hung it on the kitchen window over the sink, because I spent so much time there. She had been there for years, the Madonna, with the Child, and the lucky fish. I should explain the icon.

Icons are particular to Orthodox Christians who, unlike the Catholics, do not permit statues as objects of veneration. Instead they venerate icons, which are sacred images or representations in two-dimensional space. They are flat. Like paintings or pictures. They are holy and as commonplace in Orthodox homes as they are in churches. Icons, regardless of the medium — are "written", not painted or drawn, (though Dimitrie disagrees passionately). *Written.* The first ones appeared in catacombs where persecuted Christians hid in the 1st century. Despite two periods of iconoclasm which moved to destroy icons as if they were idols, these magnificent works have an important role in the Eastern Orthodox faith; they are, some say, windows to heaven, silent images through which the faithful can connect to the divine. One legendary origin for the icon tells of Prince Avgar who suffered from leprosy. He had begged Jesus to visit him and heal his infirmity, but the Passion was at hand, so another solution was proposed.[40] Another is the story (St.) Veronica, a woman who reputedly wiped the face of Jesus with her veil as he carried his cross. The image of Christ's face was left in the cloth. These icons are not, however, aesthetic works of art—they are more than this, as Prince Avgar attested. But St. Veronica's Veil and the Mandylion were lost and the prospect of losing my little icon loomed as devastating to me.

I pulled her from the rubbish the way one would pull a drowning child from the water. If ever I thought the Virgin would speak to me, it was then, but then I feared her reproach: *How could you let him do this to me, my child?* Icons have been known to weep, but they never, ever speak. This is why the mouths of figures in icons are always closed. *Interesting.*

When I got back to the house I collected my heart and eyes that were by now so anxious and swollen with emotion they scarcely fit back in their usual places.

He was elsewhere.

Hours passed before I could even bear to look at him. I restored her to her place by the window and took a long shower. When I saw him later that evening, I said,

"How could you do such a thing?"

My voice was hard. He stood before me absent of anything familiar. He seemed abundantly vacant and queer. I felt God shudder and a dust settled upon the obsessively clean Hungarian iconoclast like a curse.

I felt a wee bit vindicated only months later when I heard he had been deported, this, after a ten-year dalliance with immigration and appeals lawyers. Still, I continued to throw slender pointed missiles at his picture on my dart board. It was a small picture that I offset intentionally from the bull's-eye on account of the small target and my inferior aim. Plenty of holes, though. There weren't enough holes even so.

Two years later on a cold-cold night I got a most unexpected phone call.

"Janos is dead," said the man's voice.

I looked at the icon.

"What?"

"You sent him to his death," the man said with a thick angry voice.

I looked at the dart board.

"How?"

"He hanged himself. His mother found him."

He was three days shy of his birthday. What a pathetic jerk. When I told my sons that Janos was dead, one of them said, after collecting his thoughts,

"Wouldn't that be something if it a big giant dart just happened to run him through as he was walking down the street? Wouldn't it?"

Funny. Well, maybe not so much. Actually, it was funny, I mean, like a *Farside* comic. I tried to make myself feel guilty that I had thrown darts at his picture every day for a year. It didn't work. I simply took his picture down and burned it in a roaring fire, with every other picture I could find of him. Still I could not reconcile the matter in my conscious mind. I never could abide suicide especially because it's such a cowardly way of passing on your burden to someone else. Five years would pass before I would dream he was digging his fingers into my chest and I woke up gasping.

I coughed a little too.

I went outdoors as I frequently do to clear my head and gaze at the moon. At first I thought I was so shaken from my dream that I was confused as I visited the constellations, one by one. But something was disconcerting about the sky. An asymmetrical cluster of stars[41] shone brightly near the North star, resembling nothing I'd ever seen on a sky chart.

Imagine that.

Then the moon melted into a haze like an aperitif before being swallowed completely by a bone-grey cloud. The strange constellation blazed with light at its center, then vanished into the darkness.

Damned Hungarian. He used to make fun of me because I never tired of looking at the moon. He would say in that offhand way,

"I don't know why you find the moon so interesting. It is the same thing, the same moon, all the time, nothing new about it. The same."

Of course it sounded even more deprecating in Romanian, which is what we spoke to each other since Hungarian was inaccessible to me (oh, I tried to learn it, I even wrote a poem in Hungarian that I had slipped into an empty bottle for him to find, but as far as languages go, it is exclusive to the point that to speak it, you must also *be* Hungarian. Let's just say that the rules of grammar, the sound of the words, the complexity of all the nuances reserved for initiates is simply not worth the trouble. Nobody wants to be Hungarian, except Hungarians). But he hailed from Transylvania (after it had been returned to Romania from the Austro-Hungarian Empire); this meant he was a bitter Hungarian, displaced by post-World War II allied powers and cartographers, so Romanian was now compulsory (just as Hungarian had been for Romanians once). My grandparents used to speak Hungarian because they had to; their names were changed, the names of their towns and villages were changed — that is, after all, how one conquers. By language.

My grandfather, Iosif Panti, died before I was born but I remember him vividly. I saw him in the garage one day dressed in a dark suit, standing by the red lawnmower, the old-fashioned kind without motors and pull cords. It had gently bent blades, whose ends were offset in opposite ends of the horizontal carousel between two rubber wheels that cut the grass off at the knees. It whirred like subtle rolling r sounds off the tongue, and there he stood, my grandfather. I couldn't have been more than four — but it was him alright. He didn't say anything, probably because he didn't want to frighten me, so he just stood there, watching me as I ran my little finger along the edge of the lawnmower blade to clean the oily green gunk off of it. I did the same thing on a bicycle spoke one time. My sister was riding her bicycle with training wheels, and a depression in the pavement, straddled by the training wheels, prevented the back wheel from touching the ground. This allowed my sister to peddle madly while remaining stationary. When she had stopped pedaling, I noticed the oily black gunk on the spokes so naturally, I ran my little finger over the spoke when the wheel had come to a stop. All of a sudden my sister resumed her cycling and mangled my finger seven stitches worth. Most likely I would have cut myself deeper on the lawnmower blade too had my grandfather not been standing there, looking at me as though I were about to do something stupid, which I did.   When I grew up I acquired such a lawnmower in the hopes that my grandfather would show up again. I missed him terribly, having seen him just the one time.

The Hungarian and I, in any event, communicated in Romanian, and that meant very little, because it was an artificial language for him, while I was quite at home in it. Anyway, he didn't get the green card he was after. But the strange constellation — that was perfectly weird. What could it mean? *What would you say if I told you that I know what it means?* Anyway, a thick haze spread like a stain over the moon. My grandmother would say that whenever the moon is hazy it means rain. Come to think of it, on that particular night, it did feel like rain.

BOOK XIII

The Angel shivered as he sped higher and higher like a madman, while I, having no corporeal form to speak of, felt my soul peeling away from his immense and naked form, rolling backward on my essence, turning my soul inside out against the phenomenal wind shear of space. He made for the hole in the floor of Heaven with my soul caught on shoots of featherless quills like chiffon snared by nettles. On his final approach he pulled his wings taut against his body now singed with fiery flight and clasped over part of my torn and matted soul which, fortunately, totaled the center of my soul, the purest, densest part. The rest of it was forsaken and dispersed like dandelion fluff across the uni^{VERSE}.

In a burst of redemption the Angel plowed through the hole, slowed by my ragged remains billowing behind him like a forlorn parachute. He rolled, somersaulted; he tumbled, furrowing the firmament with reckless grace, displacing a long established serenity with blue-white dust and tufts of mystical[HIGGS] particles,[42] skidding to a magnificent halt at the very feet of the great God. He lay there in a tangled web of filament and fiber, strands of the Hermit's soul stretched from a thousand crushed and splintered quill stalks on his mottled wings back to the point of entry.

"You look like hell," He said, finally, in a matter of fact sort of way. "Honestly, I expected a more triumphant entrance after so many, many times."

"Forgive me, LORD," stammered the Angel, shivering and inspecting the embarrassing stubble that was still smoking, pulling gently at the strands of the Hermit's soul that popped in different tones like harp strings that snapped when they are wound too tightly. "That hole seems to get smaller and smaller."

"Indeed."

The Angel was humiliated. God was annoyed. Again. He anticipated Michael's rebuke and squinted ever so slightly in his direction. Raphael bent his head in his generous fashion and said quietly,

"I'll get the spindle."

The *spindle of forgetting* was a merciful solution to the Hermit's tragic state. Each recoverable strand was carefully wound around the spindle until it looked like a brilliant white cocoon with a stick running through it. Then God spoke a prayer of enchantment over the Hermit's newly spun soul followed by the traditional *ptui-ptui* (ritual spitting), to keep evil at bay and heal the Hermit of all manner of affliction. He said to Raphael,

"See that the Hermit has a quiet place to rest."

Raphael took the Hermit to a secluded coast with sparse vegetation and a peaceful promontory that overlooked a tranquil sea. (Surprised? There are such seas in Heaven, truly. It's written in the God's Journal). He climbed high onto the rocky outcroppings and laid the spindle out of sight, out of curiosity's reach. He drizzled oil and balsam over the Hermit's soul, propped it at the same angle as the earth's axis against a cleft in the rock, then lit a candle, which he set beside it. At the very top of the wrapped and bundled soul he twisted a few strands loose and rubbed them between his fingers over the flame so they made a crisping noise that further produced a fine wisp of smoke that dispersed a wondrous fragrance all around the Hermit.

"This will seal your sojourn until the appointed time. No harm will come to you."

The spindle slowly gave way to a wooden spine, and the spine to limbs and limbs to long slender hands and feet and all the while the Hermit slumbered. But as the organism formed and developed inside the spun soul, the brilliant white shell merged into the contours of the Hermit's back and chest, like ivory armor over ivory chainmail. When the Hermit awoke, the world was at war.

And a bloody war it was indeed. A mighty fortress with honey-colored walls and 370 towers rose above a marble sea at the apex of a great triangle that defined a city under siege.[43] The battle was fearsome, devastating, replete with carnage and spoil, valiant strife and sacrifice. Betrayal. And plunder. As the battle throbbed, blood ran like scarlet rivulets into crimson rivers, and crimson rivers into cinnabar lakes. The Hermit gleamed white then silver, the quest, specific and pure; gather as many words as could be born away in the blink of an eye. There were but two left whole: faith and sorrow, and many fragments which filled a small leather pouch. Through the blistering air of smoke — the feverish kind that comes of annihilation of precious beings, ancient manuscripts and reliquaries, the Hermit saw her, the *Blachernitissa*,[44] and pressed her to the ivory breastplate, translated[45] her there, then released her, and departed for the honey-colored wall that ran straight down to the water before plunging into the marble sea like a falling star.

BOOK XIV

You stretch out in my mind like a dock over the sea
you whisper to me, "come here," and
I climb onto the wooden boards
strung together with your voice,
so calm and certain.

Lightly I walk, gathering your words with
Every furtive footstep,
aware of the narrowness of the path
suspended
by grace, animated by your longing.

I sit quietly where your will stops;
I cast a glance back toward the strand —
The shore looks like the threshold of
infinity, while the ubiquitous sea that sees me
now youthful, murmurs to the primordial horizon.
I let my bare legs dangle over the

dock's edge, supple in their gentle swinging;
my feet skim the water without worry,
my toes dip in ripples that break like
brightening smiles.
Then I lie back and hear you
sigh through the wood beneath my
cautious weight
the breezes of hidden stars in the sky
thickened now blue race to overtake me,
making me turn my head to one side. Everything
stops abruptly,
the moment wraps me in arrested time
I – I am startled by my heart spurred;

My blouse luffs at my breast transpired
by secret burning emotions that
bead into tiny pearls of sweet oil on my skin;
my spine arcs gracefully off the dock
toward your body that covers me like a wave.
The sea rushes into my loving eyes;
I sink.[46]

BOOK XV

The Hermit had learned to walk nimbly whenever the Angel slept within, and on this particular evening a nearby village glowed with light and noise, drawing the Hermit out from the cave. The ground was cool, the brush twitched as the Hermit glided light of foot and full of anticipation. In a small leather pouched that swung from a many-colored belt around the Hermit's slender waist, two words jangled against each other.

The Angel stirred. The Hermit stood stone still, the tiny wings began beating a fragrant lullaby to soothe the cumbersome angel who commenced to snoring bye and bye, rumbling against the Hermit's stomach like hunger pangs. Just then some children happened by and spotted the rustling leaves that betrayed the Hermit's presence. Quickly the Hermit moistened the beating wings with spittle and laid them flat against a fear-sweat brow. The wings were so translucent that they nearly disappeared from view. What luck!

"Who's there?" came one voice.

"Come out where we can see you," came another.

"Show yourself," a third.

The Hermit emerged. The children took a few steps back.

"What are you doing here?"

The Hermit reflected on the curious creatures, each one different than the next; one tall, one short, one neither of the two.

"Who are you — speak up or we'll give you a beating."

At this the Hermit bristled and turned to run away, snagging the small leather pouch on a branch and in an instant vanishing into the hinter night.

The tall child heard the soft jangling and saw the pouch dangling. Eagerly he uncinched it and gazed inside then dropped the pouched as if startled and ran off with the others. Two words tumbled out:

I AM.[47]

• • •

The Hermit mined and quarried with strange verve and preoccupation. The Angel could bear it no longer and finally said,

"Who do you think you are kidding, eh? You lost them, didn't you."

"Mind your own business, old man, can't you see I am working?"

"You will not mine them a second time. Don't even bother."

"What do you know anyway?"

"Oh, this and that, and then some. I know you lost them, and I know you are afraid.

The Hermit struck at the rock displacing angry chunks of mineral that seethed gold and ore. Sweat twinkled in self- reproach; the Angel waited and perceived, waited and reflected, waited a bit longer and then said,

"I know where they are."

At this the Hermit cried out, hurling the hammer and chisel across the cave, and such was the anguished cry that the Angel spied for an instant the fair light of heaven ringing the hole in the firmament.

"Why do you torment me so?"

"Do not mistake torment for purpose, my young friend. How long do you think you would have lasted without me? Besides, I have kept you company all this time; shared mysteries with you – and taught you a thing or two besides. Why, you would rather have been tormented by ignorance and loneliness? I think not. You at least are free to experience the world around you – eh? Does this count for nothing?"

"Free? How do you suppose that I am free? I cannot fly, I cannot be with others of my own kind. And your precious mysteries — to what avail? I must slave – "

" – Serve$_{PROSKUNEO}$ "

" – Serve?"

"You must serve day and night in this cave. You are not a slave, child. You are a servant, as am I."

"If I were truly free, then should I not be free to choose whom I serve?"

"Oh, but you did, only you have forgotten."

The Hermit and the Angel fell silent for a long while, each faltering beneath the weight of faith and sorrow. Meanwhile, outside a brilliant red bird coursed the air and descended with exquisite precision to the very spot where the two words had lobbed out of the pouch, and snatched them with his feet; in his beak he carried the pouch. Then he rose like rocket and made for the top of the mountain. And the mountain rumbled. The earth shook.

An immense heat radiated through the cave and the Hermit, awash in intense burning and overcome with fear and confusion, dove into the pool of sobs and whimpers. The Angel had endured many trials, many sufferings, but water was most dangerous.

And the bush burned.

BOOK XVI

The sky was too vast for the night to fill and so my heart climbed in its purpose to dance at last among the stars this once. The flowers crowded all around in perfumed envy when he opened his arms to me. So casual he seemed and yet resigned in his invitation that I demurred at first, but quickly accepted while in the corner fire churned in the belly of a hollowed-brick gourd. The moment was more than I could afford yet too precious to lose; he would have me indeed, by moonlight and music, and I could no more choose to deny him than rejoice at such kind serendipity. He caught me close and the flowers gasped like young girls and old women baffled by such sweet anxieties as this. And I sighed and steadied my weakening resolve to remember doctrinal virtues that fled from the center of my soul like anxious butterflies seeking communion in the enchanted ether that lies between heaven and earth. Surely God would understand how a woman waxes weak when her hand rests over the heart of a man who cradles it to his chest; or leaves herself gratified at the sensation of his soft shorn beard against her cheek, the smell of his shirt, the delicate design of his ear, the blush and shudder of human form, or the passion of innocence revealed by moonlight and music. One by one the stars appeared and flickered here and whispered there among themselves with rich and sparkling curiosity over human need.

Surely He would judge that it was not the greed of desire, but rather the mortal grace of this chaste encounter. For it was never the lust of beauty or youth that crowned the moon with compassion as it spun its gentle guile between my girlish blush and his disarming smile. No. It was the stunning revelation of human touch that saves us from bitterness and confirms our humanity.

Still I could not imagine the things he thought just then when with stilted steps I counted the measure of my angst and affection — I dared not reason what might follow, for in truth, it was enough that I could breathe and swallow and sway in time with the music from the window. Some would argue that it was mere seduction, but we might agree, he and I, that it was pure confession of mutual loneliness and hunger born of isolation and fear, heartache and denial in lofty praise of strength of spirit. Surely He would know it was the honest expression of intimate community, the trinity of man, after a fashion — heart, soul and mind animated in blood, bone, and muscle, and an essence of the divine.

The fire fell asleep and the window became an icon that interceded in my search for human affirmation of God's great mercy. The music made me press closer yet until a single strand of moonlight wove its will between us, suspending the prelude of his intention to convey what had long been implied. And as if to bewitch the space between his cheek and my face, there a kiss on his breath of scattered grape escaped from his lips to mine.

Without guilt or circumspection I lingered in blessed disambiguation of that kiss and traced with my nimble fingers the warmth of his breath, vividly studying his beautiful mouth with my eager replies, taking with my eyes what I could not gather with my lips. His hands wandered in subtle provocation, stirring emotion that slumbered in places long abandoned.

It was not a time for questions or rebuke, not a moment to be spared for regret or reprisal, but an instant in which to weave linear and cyclical time into a wreath of the wonder and relief of earnest affection. But all too suddenly the moonlight and music withdrew their charming sympathy and divided us. He appeared composed though my heart would reflect in great detail every nuance, every quiver of delight, the smell of his cotton shirt misted with my perspiring touch, the taste of his eyelashes and the way he split the darkness in my soul into shimmering particles of my redemption. When next the full moon rises in the east will I remember an artist or priest?

And if in silent repose he remembers that dance would he chance to inquire of God's plan that a plain and sturdy woman should long for such a man as he? Still, if the moon, in its Gordian light should perplex my confessor with anxious phantoms, may the angels whisper a dream that shows the manner in which I propose to untie the knot that keeps him from me.

BOOK XVII

The last thing she remembered was lying down in the green-green grass in front of the rock as big as a melon into which she scarped out a hollow space. When she awoke, she was alone, but more than this, she was alone inside the cave she had fashioned on a whim that seemed nearly divine, but drifted toward the artistic. Had she not felt so consummately alone she might have been frightened to discover a veritable catacomb of words mined many creations ago; words stood out over other words that lay beneath; and different sequences of letters could be discerned based on the angle of her sight.

It was wondrous, to be sure, cryptic, incomprehensible and yet, clear and natural to behold. There, to her right, a spike struck upward from the cave floor, thick at its base and tapered to a finer point, with swirls of colors, each one dominating the sculpture in its turn. Above her, various sizes and shapes of similar spikes, each with a tear drop of quixotic minerals frozen in formation. To her left, a fire burned in an asymmetrical border of rocks whose smoke was filigree, aromatic, pleasing in every way. And finally, further back from the mouth of the cave a sad serene pool that murmured *come closer*.

As she peered into the beryl blue water her gaze was quickly arrested by another pair of eyes gazing back at her. The deeper she gazed, the better the sunken eyes came into view, and not long after, she beheld someone trapped there, in the left eye of the very one that stared up at her. Small bubbles streamed from the Hermit's mouth, each one breaking against the still face of the water, rising like sparks, some stinging her face. She brushed them away. What could this mean? Who could it be? Slowly she pushed her hand into the water so quietly that not a ripple echoed her touch. Her fingers stretched toward the creature who, deprived of air, was compelled to reach out in turn, and the instant their fingers touched, they also intertwined; she pulled the Hermit to the surface, then to the edge of the pool, feeling a terrific weight contrary to the Hermit's lithe frame.

She could drag the strange young creature no further out of the pool than waist high at first, for the body was strangely heavy, but after many hours, or so it seemed to her, she drew the Hermit little by little closer to the fire that burned in an asymmetrical arrangement of rocks. There she succumbed to fatigue and retreated to a deep sleep.

She tumbled through a myriad of memories — many of which belonged to someone else, memories she had fought against as if they were demons. She remembered one, however, that was truly hers, one around which the others orbited, each in their own ring of activity. She miscarried at five months. It started with one spot of blood.

"How much blood?"

78

"A drop."

"Red — bright red? Or dark brown?" "…Bright red."

"How big is the spot?" "Like a dime."

"Better come in."

It was a steady decline from that moment. The dime-size spot of bright red blood might just as well have been rivers of blood that ran in the sack of Constantinople. But she held fast to her will to save the pregnancy, save the child, her child.

"Doctor wants to keep you for observation."

But she refused to stay in the hospital. She argued she would stay in bed at home just as easily as she would in the hospital under observation. Besides, she knew about hospitals because she worked in a pathology lab. She hated them. She had seen too much of human tissue from a budding fetus in the serpinginous, convoluted fallopian tube in an ectopic pregnancy, to disembodied organs — eyes, livers, bowel, lungs; ovarian tumors as big as basketballs, bird shot scattered among bone fragments blown out by 12 gauge shot gun blasts, whole brains and broken hearts. The old pathologist told her once that this job would teach her humility. It did. And then some.

So they let her go with strict orders for bed rest and absolutely no moving around except to use the bathroom. Fine.

The first day was filled with anguish; she lay there, restless, preoccupied, worried. Her husband seemed aloof and went about his business in the usual way, although he did bring her dinner, which she could not eat. The next three days unfolded the same way, except that she was totally alone and at the mercy of every fear, every stray regret, every question that provoked her to reproach her sad state of mind. There were occasional phone calls, chipper voices on the other end, cheerful nonsense to fill the lulls in conversation. No more red spot. Lots of dark brown blood though.

On the fifth day around two in the afternoon, she found herself dreaming a strange dream with a great ship docked in a busy ancient port. Seven diminutive women in bright orange robes from head to foot disembarked the ship, and four re-boarded. She was aware she was dreaming and decided to awake, but instead the dream took a curious turn. She was holding in her fingers a faded trinket from a good friend that bore the patron saint of Naples — St. Gennaro. She looked at it and suddenly a fiery light burned in the center of the face, the flames curling back to the edges of the medallion and revealing another face behind it. It was the Theotokos — the *Birthgiver of God*, and it was no longer a dream for she was no longer asleep. The shining, serene face seemed bigger than the room, defying all sense of space and proportion, yet manipulating space and consciousness as if to correct reality and put things in proper perspective. She studied her for an indefinable moment and then the regular roomscape came into ordinary view.

She gasped from the starkness of the room, the ordinary light drifting in through the windows, the soft tick of the clock on the dresser, the vibration of her heart through her every cell in her body. It was still two o'clock. She called her mother. Her mother was moved — incredulous but in a faithful sort of way. She dared not suggest it might have been a dream of consolation…..okay, a vision of consolation, maybe. Her mother said she would call an old man they knew to inquire as to the meaning of the dream — okay, the meaning of the vision.

"I'll call you back."

After twenty minutes or so, the phone rang and her mother relayed the counsel of the old man. *Tell her to read the book of the Wisdom of Solomon and she will discover the meaning of the dream.* Vision.

Well, she read and read and understood nothing.

There was no revelation, no illumination, not so much as a scant suggestion. Just more dark brown blood.

She drove herself to the emergency room and there she was admitted.

St. John Hospital seemed a gentle place to be, though she was not Catholic. Saints are saints, she thought, even if they look like statues and not icons. Her husband finally arrived after she had been given the corner bed in a ward with three other wailing and grunting women. At least there were curtains. But the same way no one dared suggest she had had a dream of consolation — okay, *vision* — no one found an appropriate way to warn her that she would leave the hospital the same way she arrived. Alone. At midnight an indifferent nurse started an intravenous drip that would induce labor, explaining in a droning tone that because she was already five months pregnant, she would have to deliver the spoiled fruit of her womb. Mock labor. *Therapeutic abortion* they called it. And labor she did, all night long, strong, virulent contractions that made her molars feel they were being pulled from the inside. By dawn a terrifying gush carried a cluster of tissue and blood and tender cartilage from her, which was quickly retrieved and carried off to the pathology lab in a plastic container. Someone there would pour it onto a tray, give it a number, snap a picture and then attend the pathologist who dictated the dissection. After, the sample tissue would be processed through various chemical baths and then set into a block of wax, from which ultra thin sections would be sliced and placed on a slide, and the slide, in a warmer to melt the wax and leave the cytological print behind. Sort of like a biological icon. A window into what went wrong. The slides were then stained with other chemicals to reveal the pathology of the tissue, and a report was rendered.

She recalled a series of jars in which floated embryonic tissue from the earliest stages of development, germinating structures that were discerned through the translucent body by red and blue dye, ghostly apparitions of tiny beings who chose, or were chosen to refuse the destiny that could have awaited them. It was a moment of utter desolation for her, all the more because she was alone.

Her husband had gone to work and could not be located in time to see her before surgery. They wheeled her down to the O.R. and left her on a gurney in the hallway. Were it not for a statue of the Virgin Mary in the opposite corner, which she perceived as a flat image against the wall, she may well have lost her mind in anticipation of the aftermath of her miscarriage. The procedure that followed was one of the ugliest things she would ever recall in her life. By the way, it was a girl, they told her. *It*.

Anyone can tell you that the hardiest of souls falters in unforgiving ways when tested. And if it's true that the only compliment to immense sorrow is faith, it is equally true that grief is a fortress of honey-colored walls that go straight down into a marble sea.

She never did discover the meaning of that fantastic visitation in any text as the old man had instructed, and she shared this memory with precious few people. But she did begin to write icons from that moment on. Secretly she hoped she would have another wondrous encounter, but while she waited, she wrote icon after icon, finding a mysterious fulfillment in each one. Maybe this was the point, maybe this was the text she must read in order to discover the meaning of her dream^{VISION}. She also started to collect rocks and began building all kinds of castles and fortresses. Everyone who knew her and meant something to her had an icon and a stone house from her. She's a funny girl, that one.

Her husband did give her two fine healthy sons before he abandoned her. But whenever anyone asked her how many children she had, her first inclination was to answer three.

BOOK XVIII

A t the center of the earth the trapped kingdom pulses like a radiant heart. The first time the Angel and the Hermit, or Hermit and Angel, if you prefer, fell into the sea the power of that kingdom exerted its force with such energy that they had to yield to an extraordinary odyssey that ended where the first word began. It was a perilous journey to be sure, as are most journeys that strive homeward, such as the angel's calamitous return to Paradise. James Joyce was right: *the shortest way home is the longest way 'round.*[48] In this case, the Hermit was bound for the first Word of creation, thus the Angel had little choice in the matter.

The same seed from the forsaken apple that had left a hole in the floor of Heaven before falling from Eve's hand, made a similar hole as it burrowed into the first words. Like a comet. And anyone can tell you that comets have tails. So too the apple seed. According to divine physics, which is not based largely in theory as your physics is, the flight of the apple seed established a kind of trail or path from celestial heaven to terrestrial heaven, or in this case, sub-terrestrial heaven. On the occasion of this particular fall, a multi-colored band arced across the sky, disrupting the Angel's trajectory and diverting him and his passenger into the sea and, if that wasn't spectacular enough, establishing him precisely on the primordial trail of one inscrutable apple seed. The breathtaking velocity of this unbelievable event caused the Angel to unravel like a sweater snagged on a nail so that the Hermit thrashed behind like a threadbare sail. The first to slip into the hole of the trapped kingdom was the little butterfly (who, as you might recall, was an acknowledged stowaway of sorts), whose tiny legs were now woven around the very end of the end — or the beginning — of the angelic strand.

"I'll get the spindle."

Ptui-ptui.

This explains how the soul of the Hermit surfaced first, followed by the body, while the angel, who had sunk under the weight of gravity, remained behind in the lost kingdom for a long$^{\text{VERY LONG}}$ time, spun around the spindle of forgetting, at least until the Hermit built the fortress by the sea. The Hermit would visit those honey-colored walls much later in search of words that would recover the Angel.

What the Hermit learned the day the mountain rumbled and the earth shook, was another entrance to the trapped kingdom, a secret entrance at the bottom of the pool of sobs and whimpers, which was really an underground spring, a mystical confluence of human and divine, and then some. And what the girl perceived in the left eye of the Hermit when she drew him from the pool, was the image [ICON] of the Angel, which further explained the queer heaviness she struggled with to rescue the creature from the pool.

Some strive for heaven, others for the center of the earth; some search for the beginning of time, others for infinity. Some say the soul guides us, others claim forces of nature decide our fate. It was in this fashion the Hermit contemplated the young woman who lay sleeping on the cave floor.

And as she lay there, she dreamed of the priest, who was also an artist. She dreamed of the dance and the music from the window and the kisses and caresses that overtook them beneath an apricot colored moon. She dreamed too of his dark eyes that were bottomless but empty. It troubled her deeply that they never spoke of it—ever. Thus she was left to wonder if the meaning of the encounter was the actual event, or the fact that the event was never mentioned. Either way the meaning of it all eluded her. The priest would no doubt regret the dance and the meandering kisses; the artist would celebrate it. The priest would deny the passion that drove him, the artist would crave it once more. And yet, the man who embodied both priest and artist opted for silence—no apology, no denial, no affirmation, no explanation. This confounded her. But when she opened her eyes and saw the Hermit huddled a short distance away, back against the cave wall, knees drawn to chest and chin resting on folded arms, she felt a solidarity soothe her spirit like a warm and welcomed balm.

"Who are you?"

"I am the Hermit of this cave."

"What is your name?"

"I have no name."

"Why not?"

"It would not change things either way."

"But what do people call you then?"
"No one calls me."
"I see your point. How did you come to be in this cave?"
"I became here."
"Where is your family?"
"I have none."
"That is not possible."
"Yet here I am."
"What do you do here?"
"I mine words."
"What kind of words?"
"All kinds."
"For whom?"
"For you."
"Why?"
"Because you seek meaning in all things."

BOOK XIX

A tiny butterfly wriggled, twisted, strained against a silken cocoon that was more silver than white until it felt the rush of cool air on its delicate brow. The air was sweet like cornsilk and the light that carried the air bright and refreshing. As he emerged he felt something restrain him, a cumbersome weight that held him back. In that instant he saw his whole life flash before him and he paused. He struggled and fretted, grunted and toiled against the force that oppressed him, but little by little, his miniature head cleared the top of the cocoon. He craned his neck this way and that then hunched himself forward and pushed against the spindle with all his might until he squeezed his wings out as well. And what splendid wings they were, he thought.

Neither diaphanous nor apple-leafed, but covered with down as white as snow. He strode several paces out past the cocoon before the tips of his feathered wings were free of their spun trappings, marveling to himself how grand he must look, and oh, how many loves he would have to choose from. But when he tried to raise his wings he could not budge them from his side. It was enough he could walk at all, given the tremendous burden that impinged upon his thin architecture. *There must be some mistake,* he thought. *What is the meaning of these wings?* he questioned.

Just then an apple fell from the hand of a young maiden and rolled a ways before bowling over the dumbfounded butterfly with enormous feathered wings. What are the odds?

The apple imparted bits and pieces of knowledge to the peculiar butterfly with disproportionately large feathered wings that happened to include an obscure map dating back to when the Hermit's mother roamed the earth in order to define it. The origins of *Voroneț* blue lay here, in the trapped kingdom, in a secret mine whose vein stretched all the way to the floor of the Hermit's cave. The formation of the pool of sobs and whimpers was, of course, no accident ᴺᴼ ˢᵁᶜᴴ ᵀᴴᴵᴺᴳ. The spring that joined the cave to the kingdom was concealed until the Hermit's tears revealed the spot; the Hermit's eyes, you see, were pure Voroneț blue, and the tears that ran from the newborn found their way to their ancestral source. So when the Hermit dove into the pool the day the mountain rumbled and the earth shook, the secret vein from the cave floor to the trapped kingdom was in pure sight. But the Hermit could not fit through the narrow opening into the trapped kingdom, neither could the butterfly with his large feathered wings escape. Instead they gazed at each other — each recognizing a part of him that had been lost. They gazed in this fashion for a long moment and with such mutual, inherent longing, that the butterfly was at last assumed into the left eye of the Hermit. And thus the Angel percei-ved _ESSE EST PERCIPI_ was also captured ^TRANSLATED.

As the Hermit made for the return journey home to the cave, the leather pouch tied to the multi-colored band around the Hermit's waist snagged a drifting line of lon-gitude, pulling all and sundry back to the center of the trapped kingdom. Mercy and punishment fought over the Hermit and the Angel, each claiming what was due, while a world apart a young girl sailed a mighty ship with her father. When she had leaned over the side to mark the lines that could be seen against the brilliant blue of the sea and the glow of the lost kingdom, she had seen the Her-mit there too, torn between one kingdom and another; she saw the Hermit's life flash before her eyes — strange but true. And the Hermit saw her life flash before him, while the Angel saw the heart of God skip a beat from the left eye of the Hermit, where he swam as if flying, in the incredible forgiving blue of _Voroneţ_.

To be continued…

BOOK XX

A pocryphal tales are written by forgotten witnesses whose names are never enough. But it is the writing of the tale that gives it truth, and if not truth, then meaning. Sometimes meaning makes all the difference. When the girl swallowed a stone with a glint, she made more of it than it ever was or could be. The stone gave weight-MEANING to her fragile soul that could have otherwise lifted itself free of her and been blown to heaven just as sudden flight overtakes a butterfly who forgets to cling fast to a branch. In that same sacred space where mercy and punishment, or flying and falling dwell, in that same plane that hosts the misfit and misbegotten, sorrow and faith also have their a home, like a kingdom trapped.

Yes, the girl had recognized the Hermit, and the Hermit had recognized the girl; they sat for a very long while conversing in words mined from the cave, filling themselves with meaning until only one word was left between them.

Love.[49]

The Hermit's heart began to fill with hope and substance, swelling with the very first word from which all other words come. And the girl saw the Hermit's chest rise and fall in perfect concert with her own.

And God sigh[NAI]ed.

And the mountain slept.

And the world forgave.

So the girl dove into the right eye of the Hermit, into a sea of mystical sustaining *Voroneṭ* blue, and the force of the plunge was such that the Angel, swimming as if flying in the left eye of the Hermit burst out and exploded in the heavens into a strange new constellation, mirrored in the pattern of the asymmetrical arrangement of rocks around the fire that burned for an eternity.

All that was left of the Hermit and the girl and the Angel and the butterfly was an icon of wax and ash in the cave wall. Near it stands a spike in the form of a woman who wandered, and at her breast glows a heart that beats like the wings of a red bird.

ENDNOTES

[1] Genesis1:3.

[2] *Tohu wa bohu* (וֹהֹבָו וֹהֹת)-Genesis 1:2 as it refers to the moment preceding Creation when the world was formless and void, often translated as "welter and waste", suggesting unformedness and emptiness. Taken together, the word phrase implies a cosmic setting without function and void of creation. In the Hebrew Bible, there are three occurrences of this word pair, never appearing separate from the other.

[3] Referring to grammatical tense. Ancient Hebrew was an aspectual language, with no future tense per se, and whose verbs are not marked for tense. Therefore, one cannot determine the tense of a verb simply by looking at the spelling. The context indicates when the action occurs. Also a pun on the word *tense*.

[4] Oral language precedes the written form, therefore, words exist as sounds with implied meaning, while letters arrive much later to represent the sounds. The paradox to Genesis 1:2, is that God commands "Let there be light," which means that the word for it has been determined. The Hermit here, is mining the original word for "light," which in Hebrew is רוא (orh), but must be recovered at the level of word, and not disconnected letters.

[5] The suggestion is that the fragments of rock are precious gemstones, or pigment veins in the rock. The Hermit "brushes" the pigment into the skin, as a tattoo that mirrors a particular text, composed as it is, of word particles.

[6] A structure or formation found in a cave from mineral deposits in water, speliothem originate from the Greek *spēlaion*, meaning cave, and *thema*, for something laid down, deposit.

[7] רוא, φῶς, translate as "light" in Ancient Hebrew and Koiné, respectively.

[8] Some say this is the place where God extracted Adam's rib in the creation of Eve.

[9] When Noah sought signs to the end of the flood, he dispatched first a raven and then a dove, who returned with a sprig of an olive branch, signifying that the waters had abated, and dry land was emerging.

[10] This refers to the Romanian *ursitoare*, who upon the birth of a newborn circles the house to divine the fate of the child.

[11] The story of Jacob and Esau, sons of Isaac and grandsons of Abraham reveals that Jacob held fast to his twin brother's heel, foreshadowing his future acquisition of Esau's birthright and blessing. Genesis 25:26.

[12] Sir Isaac Newton's First Law of motion states that a moving object tends to keep moving at the same speed and in the same direction unless a force acts on it. An object at rest tends to stay at rest unless a force acts on it.

[13] George Berkeley, Bishop of Cloyne (1685-1753), was an important philosopher of the early modern period. His subjective idealism proposed an argument of immaterialism. He is famous for his proposition that *"Esse est percipi"* (To be is to be perceived). Here the suggestion is that consciousness works both ways: what the butterfly perceives exists, but God also possesses consciousness, therefore, He perceives the butterfly and all events that transpire, even if the butterfly is not particularly conscious of the same events. Such events, therefore, may result in the uncanny sensation of "déjà vu," because God's consciousness may randomly inform the unconscious subject, in this case, the butterfly.

[14] The allusion is to nourishment such as future manna from heaven. See Exodus 16:1-36, and Numbers 11:1-9. The miraculous life-saving edible substance arrived by night in the form of dew, as explained in Numbers, or hoarfrost, in Exodus, that resembled a coriander seed. It provided sustenance for the Wilderness generation as it wandered in the desert, after Moses led the Exodus from Egypt.

[15] The odour of sanctity refers to the sweet fragrance associated with the presence of saints, usually at the time of their death, or corresponding to their relics.

[16] God's signature remark in the Creation story, Genesis 1.

[17] A popular Romanian style of music, similar to an ode, thus slow, melodic, and brooding.

[18] The reference is to the amygdala, which is a complex structure in the temporal lobe of the brain. It is involved in fight or flight behavior, along with numerous other functions.

[19] The reference is to Lot's wife who turned into a pillar of salt because she looked back at the destruction of Sodom and Gomorrah, though warned not to do so. Genesis 19:26.

[20] *Tohu wa bohu*, a biblical Hebrew term found in Genesis 1 that describes the moment before Creation.

[21] Phrygian legend about a farmer named Gordias who solved the seemingly intractable problem of untying a complicated knot by cutting it with a sword.

[22] Hebrew *yovel* לבוי, the end of seven Sabbatical years. A time of great celebration.

[23] Bishop George Berkely (1685-1753), whose philosophical idealism opposed the materialism of Thomas Hobbes. His famous claim *essi est percipi*, to be perceived is to exist, is central to his argument that God exists.

[24] Refers to Einstein's thought experiment where one twin leaves earth on a spaceship that travels nearly the speed of light, and when he returns, he finds his twin has aged more than he.

[25] Genesis 28:11 records how Jacob stops for the night and takes a stone for a pillow (לְאַ תִיַב). He dreams of the ladder to heaven, and the next morning anoints the stone, naming it Beth-el (House of God). The stone reputedly stays with the Israelites until it is transferred to Ireland, then Scotland, before its sojourn in England as the Coronation Stone.

[26] A wooden board used as an instrument in the Orthodox church which, when struck with wooden hammers produces a percussive melody. A fourth century Syrian apocryphal tale *Pestera comorilor*, by Efrem the Syriac attributes the origin to Noah, who was instructed by God to beat the board three times a day to call people to repentance before the Great Flood.

[27] *Lamentation of Sofia*, in which Holy Wisdom laments the loss of man's love of wisdom.

[28] Voroneţ is a medieval monastery was founded in 1503 by Luca Arbore, the advisor of Stephen the Great *(Stefan cel Mare)*. It was painted four decades later by Dragos Coman, one of the greatest 16th century mural painters of Romania. The many frescoes feature a shade of blue that has yet to be reproduced. Popular legend, however, attributes the founding of the monastery to Stephen the Great in 1488, and names *Daniil Sihastrul* (the Hermit) the first abbot of the monastery.

[29] One of the lost manuscripts of *Sihastrul*, discovered in a cave in the Godeanu Mountains, Caraş-Severin, Romania [30] This marks the spot of the origin of the curious stalagmite in the Hermit's cave.

[31] Greek lyric poet (c. 610- c. 570), hailed by Plato as the 10th muse, of whose works very few remain.

[32] Any of several varieties of apple; the seed of a fleshy fruit: a pip; a person or thing that is admired.

[33] The Noachan Covenant refers to God's promise to Noah that He would never again destroy the world by flood. The covenant sign is the rainbow, Genesis 9:13.

[34] The ship from Book VIII.

[35] The reference here is to Book VII.

[36] The kingdom refers to the City of Byzantium, built in 7 BC and later chosen by Constantine the Great as his capital in 324, and renamed Constantinople.

[37] Refers to a popular ballad of Great Britain, where young man asks the listener to perform several impossible tasks.. It was made famous by Simon and Garfunkle, as *Are you Going to Scarbourough Fair*, released as a single in 1968.

[38] A reference to Bishop Berkley by way of jest: If you can't smell it, does it exist?

[39] The meaning here is that every live fish named Lucky died. So the fishing lure was an attempt at thwarting death: a "lucky" fish that could not die.

[40] The Image of Edessa is a holy relic consisting of a square or rectangular cloth, upon which a miraculous image of the face of Jesus was imprinted. It is considered to be the first icon in the Eastern Orthodox Church, and also known as the *Mandylion*. Prince Avgar sent an artist to paint Jesus' face, by whose image alone he believed would cure him. Christ though wiped his face with a napkin, and sent it back with the artist Ananias. Its feast day is August 16th,

and a version of its history is recorded Eusebius' *History of the Church*, (1.13.5-1.13.22). Called the icon not made by human hands,

[41] The constellated pattern mirrors the arrangement of rocks at the Hermit's cave, in which burns the fire of unknown origin.

[42] The Higgs, or Higgs Boson is a particle, or set of particles theorized as that which gives mass to other particles. It is also known as the "God particle."

[43] The battle is the Fall of Constantinople to the Turks in 1453.

[44] This is a 7th century icon of the Theotokos of Blachernae, Constantinople, which is unique among icons because it is a *bas relief* in wax, and not flat, mixed with the ashes of Christian martyrs killed in the 6th century.

[45] The term refers to moving a relic from one location to another.

[46] A psalm attributed to Hagia Sofia, found in a cave in the Godeanu Mountains.

[47] Exodus 3:14.

[48] *Ulysses*, (1922), "Think you're escaping and run into yourself. Longest way round is the shortest way home."

[49] I Corinthians 13:8-13

ABOUT THE AUTHOR

Doris Plantus is the middle daughter of an immigrant carpenter from Bucovina, and mother, whose family emigrated from Banat, Romania. She has enjoyed living in two languages and cultures her whole life, and attributes her many creative undertakings to her bilingual and bicultural experiences growing up in Detroit, Michigan. She put herself through graduate school working a variety of jobs while raising two sons, and earned her Ph.D in English, with a concentration in translation and adaptation studies. Her characteristic archaic and regionalist style in Romanian prose and poetry is a point of pride for her devoted preservation of the language she inherited and passed on to her own children. Currently she teaches a variety of courses in English at Oakland University, with a specialty in Bible as Literature. But her real passion is exploring meaning through expression, from bilingual writing, painting, iconography, sculpture, and music, to stargazing, building tree forts with her father's tools, and making wine. She lives in Troy, Michigan.